HBR Emotional Intelligence Series

How to be human at work

The HBR Emotional Intelligence Series features smart, essential reading on the human side of professional life from the pages of *Harvard Business Review*.

Empathy

Happiness

Mindfulness

Resilience

Other books on emotional intelligence from *Harvard Business Review*:

HBR's 10 Must Reads on Emotional Intelligence

HBR Guide to Emotional Intelligence

Empathy

HBR EMOTIONAL INTELLIGENCE SERIES

Empathy

HBR EMOTIONAL INTELLIGENCE SERIES

Harvard Business Review Press

Boston, Massachusetts

Library of Congress Cataloging-in-Publication Data

Title: Empathy.
Other titles: HBR emotional intelligence series.
Description: Boston, Massachusetts : Harvard Business Review Press, [2017] | Series: HBR emotional intelligence series
Identifiers: LCCN 2016056297 | ISBN 9781633693258 (pbk.)
Subjects: LCSH: Empathy. | Management.
Classification: LCC BF575.E55 E45 2017 | DDC 152.4/1—dc23 LC record available at https://lccn.loc.gov/2016056297

ISBN: 978-1-63369-325-8
eISBN: 978-1-63369-326-5

Contents

Contents

Contents

Empathy

1

What Is Empathy?

By Daniel Goleman

The word "attention" comes from the Latin *attendere*, meaning "to reach toward." This is a perfect definition of focus on others, which is the foundation of empathy and of an ability to build social relationships—the second and third pillars of emotional intelligence (the first is self-awareness).

Executives who can effectively focus on others are easy to recognize. They are the ones who find common ground, whose opinions carry the most weight, and with whom other people want to work. They emerge as natural leaders regardless of organizational or social rank.

The Empathy Triad

We talk about empathy most commonly as a single attribute. But a close look at where leaders are focusing when they exhibit it reveals three distinct kinds of empathy, each important for leadership effectiveness:

- *Cognitive empathy*: the ability to understand another person's perspective

- *Emotional empathy*: the ability to feel what someone else feels

- *Empathic concern*: the ability to sense what another person needs from you

Cognitive empathy enables leaders to explain themselves in meaningful ways—a skill essential to getting the best performance from their direct reports. Contrary to what you might expect, exercising cognitive empathy requires leaders to think about feelings rather than to feel them directly.

An inquisitive nature feeds cognitive empathy. As one successful executive with this trait puts it, "I've always just wanted to learn everything, to understand anybody that I was around—why they thought what they did, why they did what they did, what worked for them and what didn't work." But cognitive empathy is also an outgrowth of self-awareness. The executive circuits that allow us to think about our own thoughts and to monitor the feelings that flow from them let us apply the same reasoning to other people's minds when we choose to direct our attention that way.

Emotional empathy is important for effective mentoring, managing clients, and reading group dynamics. It springs from ancient parts of the brain beneath the cortex—the amygdala, the hypothalamus, the hippocampus, and the orbitofrontal cortex—that allow us to feel fast without thinking deeply. They tune us in by arousing in our bodies the emotional states of others: I literally feel your pain. My brain patterns match up with yours when I listen to you tell a gripping story. As Tania Singer, the director of the social neuroscience department at the Max Planck Institute for Human Cognitive and Brain Sciences, in Leipzig, Germany, says, "You need to understand your own feelings to understand the feelings of others." Accessing your capacity for emotional empathy depends on combining two kinds of attention: a deliberate focus on your own echoes of someone else's feelings and an open awareness of that person's face, voice, and other external signs of emotion. (See the sidebar "When Empathy Needs to Be Learned.")

WHEN EMPATHY NEEDS TO BE LEARNED

Emotional empathy can be developed. That's the conclusion suggested by research conducted with physicians by Helen Riess, the director of the Empathy and Relational Science Program at Boston's Massachusetts General Hospital. To help the physicians monitor

(Continued)

themselves, Riess set up a program in which they learned to focus using deep, diaphragmatic breathing and to cultivate a certain detachment—to watch an interaction from the ceiling, as it were, rather than being lost in their own thoughts and feelings. "Suspending your own involvement to observe what's going on gives you a mindful awareness of the interaction without being completely reactive," says Riess. "You can see if your own physiology is charged up or balanced. You can notice what's transpiring in the situation." If a doctor realizes that she's feeling irritated, for instance, that may be a signal that the patient is bothered too.

Those who are utterly at a loss may be able to prime emotional empathy essentially by faking it until they make it, Riess adds. If you act in a caring way—looking people in the eye and paying attention to their expressions, even when you don't particularly want to—you may start to feel more engaged.

Empathic concern, which is closely related to emotional empathy, enables you to sense not just how people feel but what they need from you. It's what you want in your doctor, your spouse—and your boss. Empathic concern has its roots in the circuitry that compels parents' attention to their children. Watch where people's eyes go when someone brings an adorable baby into a room, and you'll see this mammalian brain center leaping into action.

Research suggests that as people rise through the ranks, their ability to maintain personal connections suffers.

One neural theory holds that the response is triggered in the amygdala by the brain's radar for sensing danger and in the prefrontal cortex by the release of oxytocin, the chemical for caring. This implies that empathic concern is a double-edged feeling. We intuitively experience the distress of another as our own. But in deciding whether we will meet that person's needs, we deliberately weigh how much we value his or her well-being.

Getting this intuition-deliberation mix right has great implications. Those whose sympathetic feelings become too strong may themselves suffer. In the helping professions, this can lead to compassion fatigue; in executives, it can create distracting feelings of anxiety about people and circumstances that are beyond anyone's control. But those who protect themselves by deadening their feelings may lose touch with empathy. Empathic concern requires us to manage our personal distress without numbing ourselves to the pain of others. (See the sidebar "When Empathy Needs to Be Controlled.")

DANIEL GOLEMAN is a codirector of the Consortium for Research on Emotional Intelligence in Organizations at Rutgers University, coauthor of *Primal Leadership: Leading with Emotional Intelligence* (Harvard Business Review Press, 2013), and author of *The Brain and Emotional Intelligence: New Insights* and *Leadership: Selected Writings* (More Than Sound, 2011). His latest book is *A Force For Good: The Dalai Lama's Vision for Our World* (Bantam, 2015).

Excerpted from "The Focused Leader," adapted from *Harvard Business Review*, December 2013 (product #R1312B).

WHEN EMPATHY NEEDS TO BE CONTROLLED

Getting a grip on our impulse to empathize with other people's feelings can help us make better decisions when someone's emotional flood threatens to over-whelm us.

Ordinarily, when we see someone pricked with a pin, our brains emit a signal indicating that our own pain centers are echoing that distress. But physicians learn in medical school to block even such automatic responses. Their attentional anesthetic seems to be deployed by the temporal-parietal junction and re-gions of the prefrontal cortex, a circuit that boosts concentration by tuning out emotions. That's what is happening in your brain when you distance yourself from others in order to stay calm and help them. The same neural network kicks in when we see a problem in an emotionally overheated environment and need to focus on looking for a solution. If you're talking with someone who is upset, this system helps you understand the person's perspective intellectually by shifting from the heart-to-heart of emotional empathy to the head-to-heart of cognitive empathy.

What's more, some lab research suggests that the appropriate application of empathic concern is critical to making moral judgments. Brain scans have revealed that when volunteers listened to tales of people being subjected to physical pain, their own brain centers for experiencing such pain lit up instantly. But if the story was about psychological suffering, the higher brain centers involved in empathic concern and compassion took longer to activate. Some time is needed to grasp the psychological and moral dimensions of a situation. The more distracted we are, the less we can cultivate the subtler forms of empathy and compassion.

2

Why Compassion Is a Better Managerial Tactic Than Toughness

By Emma Seppala

Stanford University neurosurgeon James Doty tells the story of performing surgery on a little boy's brain tumor. In the middle of the procedure, the resident who is assisting him gets distracted and accidentally pierces a vein. With blood shedding everywhere, Doty is no longer able to see the delicate brain area he is working on. The boy's life is at stake. Doty is left with no other choice than to blindly reach into the affected area in the hopes of locating and clamping the vein. Fortunately, he is successful.

Most of us are not brain surgeons, but we certainly are all confronted with situations in which an employee makes a grave mistake, potentially ruining a critical project. The question is: How should we react when an employee is not performing well or makes a mistake?

Frustration is of course the natural response—and one we all can identify with. Especially if the mistake hurts an important project or reflects badly on us.

The traditional approach is to reprimand the employee in some way. The hope is that some form of punishment will be beneficial: It will teach the employee a lesson. Expressing our frustration also may relieve us of the stress and anger caused by the mistake. Finally, it may help the rest of the team stay on their toes to avoid making future errors.

Some managers, however, choose a different response when confronted by an underperforming employee: compassion and curiosity. Not that a part of them isn't frustrated or exasperated—maybe they still worry about how their employee's mistakes will reflect back on them—but they are somehow able to suspend judgment and may even be able to use the moment to do a bit of coaching.

What does research say is best? The more compassionate response will get you more powerful results.

First, compassion and curiosity increase employee loyalty and trust. Research has shown that feelings of warmth and positive relationships at work have a greater say over an employee's loyalty than the size of his or her paycheck.[1] In particular, a study by Jonathan Haidt of New York University shows that the more employees look up to their leaders and are moved by their compassion or kindness (a state he terms "elevation"), the more loyal they become to him or her.[2] So if you are more compassionate to your employee, not only will he or she be more loyal to you, but anyone else who has witnessed your behavior may also experience elevation and feel more devoted to you.

Conversely, responding with anger or frustration erodes loyalty. As Adam Grant, professor at the Wharton Business School and author of *Give and Take*, points out that, because of the law of reciprocity, if you embarrass or blame an employee too harshly, your reaction may end up coming around to haunt you. "Next time you need to rely on that employee, you may have lost some of the loyalty that was there before," he told me.

We are especially sensitive to signs of trustworthiness in our leaders, and compassion increases our willingness to trust.[3] Simply put, our brains respond more positively to bosses who have shown us empathy, as neuroimaging research confirms.[4] Employee trust *in turn* improves performance.[5]

Doty, who is also director of Stanford University's Center for Compassion and Altruism Research and Education, recalls his first experience in the operating room. He was so nervous that he perspired profusely. Soon enough, a drop of sweat fell into the operation site and contaminated it. The operation was a simple one, and the patients' life was in no way at stake. As for the operation site, it could have been easily irrigated. However, the operating surgeon— one of the biggest names in surgery at the time—was so angry that he kicked Doty out of the OR. Doty recalls returning home and crying tears of devastation.

Tellingly, Doty explains in an interview how, if the surgeon had acted differently, he would have gained Doty's undying loyalty. "If the surgeon, instead of raging, had said something like: 'Listen young man, look what just happened—you contaminated the field. I know you're nervous. You can't be nervous if you want to be a surgeon. Why don't you go outside and take a few minutes to collect yourself. Readjust your cap in such a way that the sweat doesn't pour down your face. Then come back and I'll show you something.' Well, then he would have been my hero forever."

Not only does an angry response erode loyalty and trust, it also inhibits creativity by jacking up the employee's stress level. As Doty explains, "Creating an environment where there is fear, anxiety, and lack of trust makes people shut down. If people have fear and anxiety, we know from neuroscience that their threat response is engaged, and their cognitive control is impacted. As a consequence, their productivity and creativity diminish." For instance, brain-imaging studies show that when we feel safe, our brain's stress response is lower.[6]

Grant also agrees that "when you respond in a frustrated, furious manner, the employee becomes less likely to take risks in the future because he or she worries about the negative consequences of making mistakes. In other words, you kill the culture of experimentation that is critical to learning and innovation." Grant refers to research by Fiona Lee at the University of Michigan that shows that promoting a culture of safety—rather than of fear of negative consequences—helps encourage the spirit of experimentation that is so critical for creativity.[7]

There is, of course, a reason we feel anger. Research shows that feelings of anger can have beneficial results. For example, they can give us the energy to stand up against injustice.[8] Moreover, they make us appear more powerful.[9] However, when as a leader you express negative emotions like anger, your employees actually view you as less effective.[10] Conversely, being likable and projecting warmth—not toughness—gives leaders a distinct advantage, as Amy Cuddy of Harvard Business School has shown.[11]

So how can you respond with more compassion the next time an employee makes a serious mistake?

1. Take a moment. Doty explains that the first thing to do is to get a handle on your own emotions—anger, frustration, or whatever the case may be. "You have to take a step back and control your own emotional response, because if you act out of emotional engagement, you are not thoughtful about your approach to the problem. By stepping back and taking a period of time to reflect, you enter a mental state that allows for a more thoughtful, reasonable, and discerned response." Practicing meditation can help improve your self-awareness and emotional control.[12]

You don't want to operate from a place where you are just pretending not to be angry. Research shows that this kind of pretense actually ends up raising heart rates for both you and your employee.[13] Instead, take some time to cool off so you can see the situation with more detachment.

2. Put yourself in your employee's shoes. Taking a step back will help give you the ability to empathize with your employee. Why was Doty, in the near-tragic moment in the operating room, able to respond productively rather than with anger? As a consequence of recalling his own first experience in the OR, he could identify and empathize with the resident. This allowed him to curb his frustration, avoid degrading the already horrified resident, and maintain the presence of mind to save a little boy's life.

The ability to perspective-take is a valuable one. Studies have shown that it helps you see aspects of the situation you may not have noticed and leads to better results in interactions and negotiations.[14] And because positions of power tend to lower our natural inclination for empathy, it is particularly important that managers have the self-awareness to make sure they practice seeing situations from their employee's perspective.[15]

3. Forgive. Empathy, of course, helps you forgive. Forgiveness not only strengthens your relationship with your employee by promoting loyalty, it turns out that it is also good for you. Whereas carrying a grudge is bad for your heart (blood pressure and heart rate both go up), forgiveness lowers both your blood pressure *and* that of the person you're forgiving.[16] Other studies show that forgiveness makes you happier and more satisfied with life, significantly reducing stress and negative emotions.[17]

When trust, loyalty, and creativity are high and stress is low, employees are happier and more productive, and turnover is lower.[18] Positive interactions even make employees healthier and require fewer sick days.[19] Other studies have shown how compassionate management leads to improvements in customer service and client outcomes and satisfaction.[20]

Doty told me he's never thrown anyone out of his OR. "It's not that I let them off the hook, but by choosing a compassionate response when they know they have made a mistake, they are not destroyed, they have learned a lesson, and they want to improve for you because you've been kind to them."

EMMA SEPPALA, PH.D., is the Science Director of Stanford University's Center for Compassion and Altruism Research and Education and author of *The Happiness Track*. She is also founder of Fulfillment Daily. Follow her on Twitter @emmaseppala or her website www.emmaseppala.com.

Notes

1. "Britain's Workers Value Companionship and Recognition Over a Big Salary, a Recent Report Revealed," AAT press release, July 15, 2014, https://www.aat.org.uk/about-aat/press-releases/britains-workers-value-companionship-recognition-over-big-salary.
2. T. Qiu et al., "The Effect of Interactional Fairness on the Performance of Cross-Functional Product Develop-

ment Teams: A Multilevel Mediated Model," *The Journal of Product Innovation Management* 26, no. 2 (March 2009): 173–187.

3. K. T. Dirks et al., "Trust in Leadership: Meta-Analytic Findings and Implications for Research and Practice," *Journal of Applied Psychology* 87, no 4 (August 2002): 611–628.

4. R. Boyatzis et al., "Examination of the Neural Substrates Activated in Memories of Experiences with Resonant and Dissonant Leaders," *The Leadership Quarterly* 23, no. 2 (April 2012): 259–272.

5. T. Bartram et al., "The Relationship between Leadership and Follower In-Role Performance and Satisfaction with the Leader: The Mediating Effects of Empowerment and Trust in the Leader," *Leadership & Organization Development Journal* 28, no. 1, (2007): 4–19.

6. L. Norman et al., "Attachment-Security Priming Attenuates Amygdala Activation to Social and Linguistic Threat," *Social Cognitive and Affective Neuroscience*, Advance Access, November 5, 2014, http://scan.oxfordjournals.org/content/early/2014/11/05/scan.nsu127.

7. F. Lee et al., "The Mixed Effects of Inconsistency on Experimentation in Organizations," *Organization Science* 15, no. 3 (2004): 310–326.

8. D. Lindebaum and P. J. Jordan, "When It Can Feel Good to Feel Bad and Bad to Feel Good: Exploring Asymmetries in Workplace Emotional Outcomes," *Human Relations*, August 27, 2014, http://hum.sagepub.com/content/early/2014/07/09/0018726714535824.full.

9. L. Z. Tiedens, "Anger and Advancement Versus Sadness and Subjugation: The Effect of Negative Emotion Expressions on Social Status Conferral," *Journal of Personality and Social Psychology* 80, no. 1 (January 2001): 86–94.

10. K. M. Lewis, "When Leaders Display Emotion: How Followers Respond to Negative Emotional Expression of Male and Female Leaders," *Journal of Organizational Behavior* 21, no. 1 (March 2000): 221–234.

11. E. Seppala, "The Hard Data on Being a Nice Boss," *Harvard Business Review*, November 24, 2014, https://hbr.org/2014/11/the-hard-data-on-being-a-nice-boss; and A. J. C. Cuddy et al., "Connect, Then Lead," *Harvard Business Review* (July–August 2013).

12. "Know Thyself: How Mindfulness Can Improve Self-Knowledge," Association for Psychological Science, March 14, 2013, http://www.psychologicalscience.org/index.php/news/releases/know-thyself-how-mindfulness-can-improve-self-knowledge.html.

13. E. Butler et al., "The Social Consequences of Expressive Suppression," *Emotion* 3, no. 1 (2013): 48–67.

14. A. Galinsky, et al., "Why It Pays to Get Inside the Head of Your Opponent: The Differential Effects of Perspective Taking and Empathy in Negotiations," *Psychological Science* 19, no. 4 (April 2008): 378–384.

15. L. Solomon, "Becoming Powerful Makes You Less Empathetic," *Harvard Business Review*, April 21, 2015, https://hbr.org/2015/04/becoming-powerful-makes-you-less-empathetic.

16. P. A. Hannon et al., "The Soothing Effects of Forgiveness on Victims' and Perpetrators' Blood Pressure," *Personal Relationships* 19, no. 2 (June 2012): 279–289.

17. G. Bono et al., "Forgiveness, Feeling Connected to Others, and Well-Being: Two Longitudinal Studies," *Personality and Social Psychology Bulletin* 34, no. 2 (February 2008): 182–195; and K. A. Lawler, "The Unique Effects of Forgiveness on Health: An Exploration of Pathways," *Journal of Behavioral Medicine* 28, no. 2 (April 2005): 157–167.

18. American Psychological Association, "By the Numbers: A Psychologically Healthy Workplace Fact Sheet," *Good Company Newsletter*, November 20, 2013, http://www.apaexcellence.org/resources/goodcompany/newsletter/article/487.

19. E. D. Heaphy and J. E. Dutton; "Positive Social Interactions and the Human Body at Work: Linking Organizations and Physiology," *Academy of Management Review* 33, no. 1 (2008): 137–162; and S. Azagba and M. Sharaf, "Psychosocial Working Conditions and the Utilization of Health Care Services," *BMC Public Health* 11, no. 642 (2011).

20. S. G. Barsdale and D. E. Gibson, "Why Does Affect Matter in Organizations?" *Academy of Management Perspectives* 21, no. 1 (February 2007): 36–59; and S. G. Barsdale and O. A. O'Neill, "What's Love Got to Do with It? A Longitudinal Study of the Culture of Companionate Love and Employee and Client Outcomes in the Long-Term

Care Setting," *Administrative Science Quarterly* 59, no. 4 (December 2014): 551–598.

Adapted from content posted on hbr.org
on May 7, 2015 (product #H021MP).

3

What Great Listeners Actually Do

By Jack Zenger and Joseph Folkman

Chances are you think you're a good listener. People's appraisal of their listening ability is much like their assessment of their driving skills, in that the great bulk of adults think they're above average.

In our experience, most people think good listening comes down to doing three things:

- Not talking when others are speaking

- Letting others know you're listening through facial expressions and verbal sounds ("Mm-hmm")

- Being able to repeat what others have said, practically word for word

In fact, much management advice on listening suggests that people should do these very things—encouraging listeners to remain quiet, nod and "mm-hmm" encouragingly, and then repeat back to the talker something like, "So, let me make sure I understand. What you're saying is . . ." However, recent research that we've conducted suggests that these behaviors fall far short of describing good listening skills.

We analyzed data that describes the behavior of 3,492 participants in a development program designed to help managers become better coaches. As part of this program, participants' coaching skills were evaluated through 360-degree assessments. We identified the individuals who were perceived as being the most effective listeners (the top 5%). We then compared the best listeners with the average of all other people in the data set and identified the 20 characteristics that seemed to set them apart. With those results in hand we identified the factors that differed between great and average listeners and analyzed the data to determine which characteristics their colleagues identified as the behaviors that made them outstanding listeners.

We found some surprising characteristics, along with some qualities we expected to hear. We grouped them into four main findings:

- *Good listening is much more than being silent while the other person talks.* To the contrary, people perceive the best listeners to be those who periodically ask questions that promote discovery and insight. These questions gently challenge old assumptions but do so in a constructive way. Sitting there silently nodding does not provide sure evidence that a person is listening, but asking a good question tells the speaker the listener has not only heard what was said but that they comprehended it well enough to want additional information. Good listening was consistently seen as a two-way dialogue, rather than a one-way "speaker versus hearer" interaction. The best conversations were active.

- *Good listening includes interactions that build up a person's self-esteem.* The best listeners make the conversation a positive experience for the other party, which doesn't happen when the listener is passive (or critical, for that matter). Good listeners make the other person feel supported and convey confidence in the speaker. Good listening is characterized by the creation of a safe environment in which issues and differences can be discussed openly.

- *Good listening is seen as a cooperative conversation.* In the interactions we studied, feedback flowed smoothly in both directions with neither party becoming defensive about comments the other made. By contrast, poor listeners were seen as competitive—as listening only to identify errors in reasoning or logic, using their silence as a chance to prepare their next response. That might make you an excellent debater, but it doesn't make you a good listener. Good listeners may challenge assumptions and disagree, but the person being listened to feels the listener is trying to help rather than trying to win an argument.

- *Good listeners tend to make suggestions.* In the study, good listening invariably included some feedback that was provided in a way others would accept and that opened up alternative paths to consider. This finding somewhat surprised us, since it's not uncommon to hear complaints that "So-and-so didn't listen, he just jumped in and tried to solve the problem." Perhaps what the data is telling us is that making suggestions is not itself the problem; it may be more about the skill with which those suggestions are made. Another possibility is that we're more likely to accept suggestions from people we already think are good listeners. (Someone who is silent for the whole conversation and then jumps in with a suggestion may not be seen as credible. Someone who seems combative or critical and then tries to give advice may not be seen as trustworthy.)

While many of us may think of being a good listener like being a sponge that accurately absorbs what the other person is saying, what these findings show is that instead, good listeners are like trampolines: You can bounce ideas off of them, and rather than absorbing your ideas and energy, they amplify, energize, and clarify your thinking. They make you feel better not by merely passively absorbing, but by actively supporting. This lets you gain energy and height, just like a trampoline.

Of course, there are different levels of listening. Not every conversation requires the highest levels of listening, but many conversations would benefit from greater focus and listening skill. Consider which level of listening you'd like to aim for.

> *Level 1*: The listener creates a safe environment in which difficult, complex, or emotional issues can be discussed.

> *Level 2*: The listener clears away distractions like phones and laptops, focusing attention on the other person and making appropriate eye contact. (This behavior not only affects how you are perceived as the listener; it immediately influences the listener's *own* attitudes and inner feelings. Acting the part changes how you feel inside. This in turn makes you a better listener.)

> *Level 3*: The listener seeks to understand the substance of what the other person is saying.

They capture ideas, ask questions, and restate issues to confirm that their understanding is correct.

Level 4: The listener observes nonverbal cues, such as facial expressions, perspiration, respiration rates, gestures, posture, and numerous other subtle body language signals. It is estimated that 80% of what we communicate comes from these signals. It sounds strange to some, but you listen with your eyes as well as your ears.

Level 5: The listener increasingly understands the other person's emotions and feelings about the topic at hand and identifies and acknowledges them. The listener empathizes with and validates those feelings in a supportive, nonjudgmental way.

Level 6: The listener asks questions that clarify assumptions the other person holds and helps the other person see the issue in a new light. This could include the listener injecting some thoughts and ideas about the topic that could be useful to the other person. However, good listeners never highjack the conversation so that they or their issues become the subject of the discussion.

Each of the levels builds on the others; thus, if you've been criticized for offering solutions rather than listening, it may mean you need to attend to some of the other levels (such as clearing away distractions or empathizing) before your proffered suggestions can be appreciated.

We suspect that in being a good listener, most of us are more likely to stop short rather than go too far. Our hope is that this research will help by providing a new perspective on listening. We hope those who labor under an illusion of superiority about their listening skills will see where they really stand. We also hope the common perception that good listening is mainly about acting like an absorbent sponge will wane. Finally, we hope all will see that the highest and best form of listening comes in playing the same role for the other person that a trampoline would play for a child: It gives energy, acceleration, height, and amplification. These are the hallmarks of great listening.

JACK ZENGER is the CEO and JOSEPH FOLKMAN is President of Zenger Folkman, a leadership development consultancy. They are coauthors of the October 2011 HBR article "Making Yourself Indispensable" and the book *How to Be Exceptional: Drive Leadership Success by Magnifying Your Strengths* (McGraw-Hill, 2012).

Adapted from content posted on hbr.org
on July 14, 2016 (product #H030DC).

4

Empathy Is Key to a Great Meeting

By Annie McKee

Yes, we all hate meetings. Yes, they are usually a waste of time. And yes, they're here to stay. So it's your responsibility as a leader to make them better. This doesn't mean just making them shorter, more efficient, and more organized. People need to enjoy them and, dare I say it, have fun.

Happiness matters a lot at work. How could it not, when many of us spend most of our waking hours there. The alternatives—chronic frustration, discontent, and outright hatred of our jobs—are simply not acceptable. Negative feelings interfere with creativity and innovation, not to mention collaboration.[1] And let's face it: Meetings are, for the most part, still where lots of collaboration, creativity, and innovation happen.[2] If meetings aren't working, then chances are we're not able to do what we need to do.

So how do we fix meetings so they are more enjoyable and produce more positive feelings? Sure, invite the right people, create better agendas, and be better prepared. Those are baseline fixes. But if you really want to improve how people work together at meetings, you'll need to rely on—and maybe develop—a couple of key emotional intelligence competencies: empathy and emotional self-management.

Why empathy? Empathy is a competency that allows you to read people. Who is supporting whom? Who is pissed off, and who is coasting? Where is the resistance? This isn't as easy as it seems. Sometimes, the smartest resisters often look like supporters, but they're not supportive at all. They're smart, sneaky idea killers.

Carefully reading people will also help you understand the major and often hidden conflicts in the group. Hint: These conflicts probably have nothing to do with the topics discussed or decisions being made at the meeting. They are far more likely to be linked to very human dynamics like who is allowed to influence whom (headquarters vs. the field, expats vs. local nationals) and power dynamics between genders and among people of various races.

Empathy lets you see and manage these power dynamics. Many of us would like to think that these sorts of concerns—and office politics in general—are beneath us, unimportant, or just for those Machiavellian folks we all dislike. Realistically, though, power is hugely important in groups because it is the real currency in most organizations. And it plays out in meetings. Learning to read how the flow of power is moving and shifting can help you lead the meeting—and everything else.

Keep in mind that employing empathy will help you understand how people are responding to *you*. As a leader you may be the most powerful person at the meeting. Some people, the dependent types, will defer at every turn. That feels good, for a minute. Carry on that way, and you're likely to create a dependent group—or one that is polarized between those who will do anything you want and those who will not.

This is where emotional self-management comes in, for a couple of reasons. First, take a look at the dependent folks in your meetings. Again, it can feel really good to have people admire you and agree with your every word. In fact, this can be a huge relief in our conflict-ridden organizations. But again, if you don't manage your response, you will make group dynamics worse. You will also look like a fool. Others are reading the group, too, and they will rightly read that you like it when people go along with you. They will see that you are falling prey to your own ego or to those who want to please or manipulate you.

Second, strong emotions set the tone for the entire group. We take our cue from one another about how to feel about what's going on around us. Are we in danger? Is there cause for celebration? Should we be fed up and cynical or hopeful and committed? Here's why this matters in meetings: If you, as a leader, effectively project out your more positive emotions, such as hope and enthusiasm, others will "mirror" these feelings and the general tone of the group will be marked by optimism and a sense of "we're in this together, and we can do it."[3] And there is a strong neurological link between feelings and cognition. We think more clearly and more creatively when our feelings are largely positive and when we are appropriately challenged.[4]

The other side of the coin is obvious. Your negative emotions are also contagious, and they are almost always destructive if unchecked and unmanaged. Express anger, contempt, or disrespect, and you will definitely push people into fight mode—individually and collectively. Express disdain, and you'll alienate people far beyond the end of the meeting. And it doesn't matter who you feel this way about. All it takes is for people to see it, and they will catch it—and worry that next time your target will be them.

This is not to say that all positive emotions are good all the time or that you should never express negative emotions. The point is that the leader's emotions are highly infectious. Know this and manage your feelings accordingly to create the kind of environment where people can work together to make decisions and get things done.

It may go without saying, but you can't do any of this with your phone on. As Daniel Goleman shares in his book *Focus: The Hidden Driver of Excellence*, we are not nearly as good at multitasking as we think we are. Actually we stink at it. So turn it off and pay attention to the people you are with today.

In the end, it's your job to make sure people leave your meeting feeling pretty good about what's happened, their contributions, and you as the leader. Empathy allows you to read what's going on, and self-management helps you move the group to a mood that supports getting things done—and happiness.

ANNIE MCKEE is a senior fellow at the University of Pennsylvania, director of the PennCLO Executive Doctoral Program, and the founder of the Teleos Leadership Institute. She is the coauthor, with Daniel Goleman and Richard Boyatzis, of *Pri-*

mal Leadership (Harvard Business Review Press, 2013) as well as a coauthor of *Resonant Leadership* (Harvard Business Review Press, 2005) and *Becoming a Resonant Leader* (Harvard Business Review Press, 2008). Her new book, *How to Be Happy at Work*, is forthcoming from Harvard Business Review Press.

Notes

1. D. Goleman et al., *Primal Leadership: Unleashing the Power of Emotional Intelligence* (rev. ed.) (Boston: Harvard Business Review Press, 2013).
2. K. D'Costa, "Why Do We Need to Have So Many Meetings?" *Scientific American*, November 17, 2014, https://blogs.scientificamerican.com/anthropology-in-practice/why-do-we-need-to-have-so-many-meetings/.
3. V. Ramachandran, "The Neurons That Shaped Civilization," TED talk, November 2009, https://www.ted.com/talks/vs_ramachandran_the_neurons_that_shaped_civilization?language=en.
4. M. Csikzsentmihalyi, *Creativity: Flow and the Psychology of Discovery and Invention* (New York: Harper Perennial, 1997).

Adapted from content posted on hbr.org
on March 23, 2015 (product #H01YDY).

5

It's Harder to Empathize with People If You've Been in Their Shoes

By Rachel Ruttan, Mary-Hunter McDonnell, and Loran Nordgren

magine that you have just become a new parent. Overwhelmed and exhausted, your performance at work is suffering. You desperately want to work from home part time to devote more attention to your family. One of your supervisors has had children while climbing the corporate ladder, while the other hasn't. Which supervisor is more likely to embrace your request?

Most people would recommend approaching the supervisor who has children, drawing on the intuition that shared experience breeds empathy. After all, she has "been there" and thus would seem best placed to understand your situation.

Our recent research suggests that this instinct is very often wrong.[1]

In a series of recent experiments, we found that people who have endured challenges in the past (like divorce or being skipped over for a promotion) were less likely to show compassion for someone facing the same struggle, compared with people with no experience in that particular situation.

In the first experiment, we surveyed people participating in a "polar plunge": a jump into a very icy Lake Michigan in March. All participants read a story about a man named Pat who intended to complete the plunge but chickened out and withdrew from the event at the last minute. Critically, participants read about Pat either before they had completed the plunge themselves or one week after. We found that polar plungers who had successfully completed the plunge were less compassionate and more contemptuous of Pat than were those who had not yet completed the plunge.

In another study, we looked at compassion toward an individual struggling with unemployment. More than 200 people read a story about a man who—despite his best efforts—is unable to find a job. Struggling to make ends meet, the man ultimately stoops to selling drugs in order to earn money. We found that people who had overcome a period of unemployment in the past were less compassionate and more judgmental of the man than people who were currently unemployed or had never been involuntarily unemployed.

A third study examined compassion toward a bullied teenager. Participants were told either that the teen was successfully coping with the bullying or that he failed to cope by lashing out violently. Compared with participants who had no experience with bullying, participants who reported having been bullied in the past themselves were more compassionate toward the teen who was appropriately coping with the experience. But, as in our earlier studies, participants who were bullied in the past were the *least* compassionate toward the teen who failed to successfully cope with the bullying.

Taken together, these results suggest that people who have endured a difficult experience are particularly likely to penalize those who struggle to cope with a similar ordeal.

But why does this occur? We suggest that this phenomenon is rooted in two psychological truths.

First, people generally have difficulty accurately recalling just how difficult a past aversive experience was. Though we may remember that a past experience was painful, stressful, or emotionally trying, we tend to underestimate just how painful that experience felt in the moment. This phenomenon is called an "empathy gap."[2]

Second, people who have previously overcome an aversive experience know that they were able to successfully overcome it, which makes them feel especially confident about their understanding of just how difficult the situation is. The combined experience of "I can't recall how difficult it was" and "I know that I got through it myself" creates the perception that the event can be readily conquered, reducing empathy toward others struggling with the event.

This finding seems to run counter to our intuitions. When we asked participants to predict who would show the most compassion for the bullied teenager, for instance—a teacher who'd endured bullying himself or one who never had—an overwhelming 99 out of the 112 people chose the teacher who had been bullied. This means that many people may be instinctively seeking compassion from the very people who are least likely to provide it.

This clearly has implications for peer-to-peer office communication (choose the person you vent to carefully). And mentorship programs, which often pair people from similar backgrounds or experiences, may need to be reexamined. But there are also important lessons for leaders. When approached by employees in distress, leaders may believe that their own emotional reaction to the issue should guide their response. For example, an executive who broke the glass ceiling may focus on her own success when considering an employee's concerns about discrimination. Similarly, managers in overworked industries such as consulting and banking may respond to employees' concerns about burnout and fatigue with comments such as, "I had to work those hours, so why are you complaining?" (And in fact, there is some evidence that this mechanism is at play when older workers push back on reforms designed to help cut down on overwork.)[3]

Simply put, leaders need to get outside of their own heads—to place *less* emphasis, not more, on their own past challenges. To bridge the empathy gap, leaders may be best served by focusing on how upset the other person seems to be or by reminding themselves that many others struggle with the same challenge. Returning to the opening example, the supervisor approached by an exhausted new parent could instead think about the countless other new parents who struggle to find work-life balance, many of whom are ultimately pushed out of the workplace.

When we're trying to encourage someone to be more empathetic, we often say something like, "walk a mile in his shoes." As it turns out, that may be exactly the wrong thing to say to people who have worn those shoes themselves.

RACHEL RUTTAN is a doctoral student at the Kellogg School of Management. MARY-HUNTER MCDONNELL is an assistant professor of management at the Wharton School. LORAN NORDGREN is an associate professor of management and organizations at the Kellogg School of Management.

Notes

1. R. L. Ruttan et al., "Having 'Been There' Doesn't Mean I Care: When Prior Experience Reduces Compassion for Emotional Distress," *Journal of Personality and Social Psychology* 108, no. 4 (April 2015): 610–622.

2. L. F. Nordgren et al., "Visceral Drives in Retrospect: Explanations About the Inaccessible Past," *Psychological Science* 17, no. 7 (July 2006): 635–640.

3. K. C. Kellogg, *Challenging Operations: Medical Reform and Resistance in Surgery* (Chicago: University of Chicago Press, 2011).

Adapted from content posted on hbr.org on
October 20, 2015 (product #H02FKN).

6

Becoming Powerful Makes You Less Empathetic

By Lou Solomon

ast year, I worked with a senior executive—let's call him Steve—who had received feedback from his boss that he was wearing the power of his new title in an off-putting way. Steve's boss told him that he had developed a subtle way of being right in meetings that sucked all the oxygen out of the room. No one wanted to offer ideas once Steve had declared the right answer. Since his promotion, Steve had become less of a team player and more of a superior who knew better than others. In short, he had lost his empathy.

Why does this sort of shift in behavior happen to so many people when they're promoted to the ranks of management? Research shows that personal power actually interferes with our ability to empathize. Dacher Keltner, an author and social psychologist at the University of California, Berkeley, has conducted empirical studies showing that people who have power suffer deficits in empathy, the ability to read emotions, and the ability to adapt behaviors to other people. In fact, power can actually change how the brain functions, according to research from Sukhvinder Obhi, a neuroscientist at Wilfrid Laurier University in Ontario, Canada.[1]

The most common leadership failures don't involve fraud, the embezzlement of funds, or sex scandals. It's more common to see leaders fail in the area of every day self-management—and the use of power in a way that is motivated by ego and self-interest.

How does it happen? Slowly, and then suddenly. It happens with bad mini choices, made perhaps on an unconscious level. It might show up as the subtle act of throwing one's weight around. Demands for special treatment, isolated decision making, and getting one's way. Leaders who are pulled over by the police for speeding or driving drunk become indignant and rail, "Do you know who I am?" Suddenly the story hits social media, and we change our minds about the once-revered personality.

This points to a bigger story about power and fame. How do people start out in pursuit of a dream and wind up aggrandizing themselves instead? They reach a choke point, where they cross over from being generous with their power to using their power for their own benefit.

Take the case of former Charlotte, North Carolina, mayor Patrick Cannon. Cannon came from nothing. He overcame poverty and the violent loss of his father at the age of 5. He earned a degree from North Carolina A&T State University and entered public service at the age of 26, becoming the youngest council member in Charlotte history. He was known for being completely committed to serving the public and generous with the time he spent as a role model for young people.

But in 2014, Cannon, then 47, pleaded guilty to accepting $50,000 in bribes while in office.[2] As he entered the city's federal courthouse, he tripped and fell. The media was there to capture the fall, which was symbolic of the much bigger fall of an elected leader and small business owner who once embodied the very essence of personal achievement against staggering odds. Cannon now has the distinction of being the first mayor in the city's history to be sent to prison. Insiders say he was a good man but all too human, and he seemed vulnerable as he became isolated in his decision making. And while a local minister argued that Cannon's one lapse in judgment should not define the man and his career of exceptional public service, he is now judged only by his weakness: his dramatic move from humility and generosity to corruption. And that image of Cannon tripping on his way into court is now the image that people associate with him.

What can leaders do if they fear that they might be crossing the line from power to abuse of power? First, you must invite other people in. You must be willing to risk vulnerability and ask for feedback. A good executive coach can help you return to a state of empathy and value-driven decisions. However, be sure to ask for feedback from a wide variety of people. Dispense with the softball questions (How am I doing?) and ask the tough ones (How does my style and focus affect my employees?).

Preventive maintenance begins with self-awareness and a daring self-inventory. Here are some important questions to ask yourself:

1. Do you have a support network of friends, family, and colleagues who care about you without the title and can help you stay down-to-earth?

2. Do you have an executive coach, mentor, or confidant?

3. What feedback have you gotten about not walking the talk?

4. Do you demand privileges?

5. Are you keeping the small, inconvenient promises that fall outside of the spotlight?

6. Do you invite others into the spotlight?

7. Do you isolate yourself in the decision-making process? Do the decisions you're making reflect what you truly value?

8. Do you admit your mistakes?

9. Are you the same person at work, at home, and in the spotlight?

10. Do you tell yourself there are exceptions or different rules for people like you?

If a leader earns our trust, we hold them to non-negotiable standards. Nothing will blow up more dramatically than a failure to walk the talk or the selfish abuse of power. We all want our leaders to be highly competent, visionary, take-charge people. However, empathy, authenticity, and generosity are what distinguish competence and greatness. The most self-aware leaders recognize the signals of abuse of power and correct course before it's too late.

LOU SOLOMON is the CEO of Interact, a communications consultancy. She is the author of *Say Something Real* and an adjunct faculty member at the McColl School of Business at Queens University of Charlotte.

Notes

1. J. Hogeveen et al., "Power Changes How the Brain Responds to Others," *Journal of Experimental Psychology* 143, no. 2 (April 2014): 755–762.
2. M. Gordon et al., "Patrick Cannon Pleads Guilty to Corruption Charge," *The Charlotte Observer*, June 3, 2014, www.charlotteobserver.com/news/local/article9127154 .html.

Adapted from content posted on hbr.org
on April 21, 2015 (product #H020S0).

7

A Process for Empathetic Product Design

By Jon Kolko

The discipline of product management is shifting from an external focus on the market, or an internal focus on technology, to an empathetic focus on people. While it's not too difficult to rally people around this general idea, it can be hard at first to understand how to translate it into tactics. So in this article, I'll walk through how we applied this approach to a particular product at a startup and how it led to large-scale adoption and, ultimately, the acquisition of the company.

I was previously VP of design at MyEdu, where we focused on helping students succeed in college, show their academic accomplishments, and gain employment. MyEdu started with a series of free academic planning tools, including a schedule planner. As we formalized a business model focused on college recruiting, we conducted behavioral, empathetic research with college students and recruiters. This type of qualitative research focuses on what people do, rather than what they say. We spent hours with students in their dorm rooms, watching them do their homework, watch TV, and register for classes. We watched them being college students, and our goal was not to identify workflow conflicts or utilitarian problems to solve; it was to build a set of intuitive feelings about what it means to be a college student. We conducted the same form of research with recruiters, watching them speak to candidates and work through their hiring process.

This form of research is misleadingly simple—you go and watch people. The challenge is in forging a disarming relationship with people in a very short period of time. Our goal is to form a master and apprentice relationship: We enter these research activities as a humble apprentice, expecting to learn from a master. It may sound a little funny, but college students are masters of being in academia, with all of the successes and failures this experience brings them.

As we complete our research, we transcribe the session in full. This time-consuming effort is critical, because it embeds the participants' collective voice in our heads. As we play, type, pause, and rewind our recordings, we begin to quite literally think from the perspective of the participant. I've found that I can repeat participant quotes and "channel" their voices years after a research session is over. We distribute the transcriptions into thousands of individual utterances, and then we post the utterances all over our war room.

The input of our behavioral research is a profile of the type of people we want to empathize with. The output of our research is a massive data set of verbatim utterances, exploded into individual, moveable parts.

Once we've generated a large quantity of data, our next step is to synthesize the contents into meaningful insights. This is an arduous, seemingly endless process—it will quite literally fill any amount of time you allot to it. We read individual notes, highlight salient points, and move the notes around. We build groups of notes in a bottom-up fashion, identifying similarities and anomalies. We invite the entire product team to participate: If they have 15 or 30 minutes, they are encouraged to pop in, read some notes, and shift them to places that make sense. Over time, the room begins to take shape. As groupings emerge, we give them action-oriented names. Rather than using pithy category labels like "Career Service" or "Employment," we write initial summary statements like "Students write résumés in order to find jobs."

When we've made substantial progress, we begin to provoke introspection on the categories by asking "why"-oriented questions. And the key to the whole process is that we answer these questions *even though we don't know the answer for sure.* We combine what we know about students with what we know about ourselves. We build on our own life experiences, and as we leverage our student-focused empathetic lens, we make inferential leaps. In this way, we drive innovation and simultaneously introduce risk. In this case, we asked the question, "Why do students develop résumés to find jobs?" and answered it, "Because they think employers want to see a résumé." This is what Roger Martin refers to as "abductive reasoning": a form of logical recombination to move past the expected and into the provocative world of innovation.[1]

Finally, when we've answered these "why" questions about each group, we create a series of insight statements, which are provocative statements of truth about human behavior. We'll build upon the why statement, abstracting our answer away from the students we spent time with and making a generalization about *all* students. We asked, "Why do students develop résumés to find jobs?" and we answered it, "Because they think employers want to see a résumé." Now we'll craft an insight statement: "Students think they have an idea of what employers want in a candidate, but they are often wrong." We've shifted from a passive statement to an active assertion. We've made a large inferential leap. And we've arrived at the scaffold for a new product, service, or idea.

We can create a similar provocative statement of truth about recruiters by learning from employers. Based on our research, we identified that recruiters spend very little time with each résumé but have very strong opinions about candidates. Our insight statement becomes "Recruiters make snap judgments, directly impacting a candidate's chances of success." (See table 1.)

The input of our synthesis process is the raw data from research, transcribed and distributed on a large wall. The output of our synthesis process is a series of insights: provocative statements of truth about human behavior.

TABLE 1

Student insight	Employer insight
Students think they have an idea of what employers want in a candidate, but they are often wrong.	**Recruiters make snap judgments, directly impacting a candidate's chances of success.**
"Your résumé is like your life: It is your golden ticket to the chocolate factory."—*Samantha, international business major*	"Don't apply to five of my jobs, because you aren't going to get any of them."—*Meg, recruiter*
<ul><li>Emphasize bullets on a résumé rather than exhibit skills through artifacts (portfolio)</li><li>Think they should have a broad but shallow set of abilities rather than a depth of competency in one area</li><li>Typically apply for any and every job</li></ul>	<ul><li>Form an opinion in seconds based on a single data point</li><li>Are looking for specific skills and evidence of competency in that skill</li><li>Create a mental narrative of what a candidate can do based on how the student presents herself</li></ul>

Now we can start to merge and compare insights in order to arrive at a value proposition. As we connect the two insights from students and employers and juxtapose them, we can narrow in on a "what-if" opportunity. What if we taught students new ways to think about finding a job? What if we showed students alternative paths to jobs? What if we helped students identify their skills and present them to employers in a credible way? (See table 2.)

If we subtly shift the language, we arrive at a capability value proposition: "MyEdu helps students identify their skills and present them to employers in a credible way."

This value proposition is a promise. We promise to students that if they use our products, we'll help them identify their skills and show those skills to employers. If we fail to deliver on that promise, students have a poor experience with our products—and leave. The same is true for any product or service company. If Comcast promises to deliver internet access to our

TABLE 2

Student insight	Employer Insight
Students think they have an idea of what employers want in a candidate, but they are often wrong.	Recruiters make snap judgments, directly impacting a candidate's chances of success.

What-if opportunity:
What if we helped students identify their skills and present them to employees in a credible way?

home but doesn't, we get frustrated. If they fail frequently enough, we dump them for a company with a similar or better value proposition.

Insights act as the input to this phase in the empathetic design process, and the output of this process is an emotionally charged value promise.

Armed with a value proposition, we have constraints around what we're building. In addition to providing an external statement of value, this statement also indicates how we can determine if the capabilities, features, and other details we brainstorm are appropriate to include in the offering. If we dream up a new feature and it doesn't help students identify their skills and present them to employers in a credible way, it's not appropriate for us to build. The value promise becomes the objective criteria in a subjective context, acting as a sieve through which we can pour our good ideas.

Now we tell stories—what we call "hero flows," or the main paths through our products that help people become happy or content. These stories paint a picture of how a person uses our product to receive the value promise. We write these, draw them as stick figures, and start to sketch the real product interfaces. And then, through a fairly standard product development process, we bring these stories to life with wireframes, visual comps, motion studies, and other traditional digital product assets.

Through this process, we developed the MyEdu Profile: a highly visual record that helps students highlight academic accomplishments and present them to employers in the context of recruiting.

During research, we heard from some college students that "LinkedIn makes me feel dumb." They don't have a lot of professional experiences, so asking them to highlight these accomplishments is a nonstarter. But as students use our academic planning tools, their behavior and activities translate to profile elements that highlight their academic accomplishments: We can deliver on our value proposition.

Our value proposition acts as the input to the core of product development. The output of this process is our products, which facilitate the iterative, incremental set of capabilities that shift behavior and help people achieve their wants, needs, and desires.

The LinkedIn example we highlighted illustrates what we call "empathetic research." We marinated in data and persevered through a rigorous process of sense making in order to arrive at insights. We leveraged these insights to provoke a value proposition, and then we built stories on top of the entire scaffold. And as a result of this process, we created a product with emotional resonance. The profile product attracted more than a million college students in about a year, and during a busy academic registration period, we saw growth of between 3,000 to 3,500 new student profiles a day. After we were acquired by education software company Blackboard and integrated this into the flagship learning management system, we saw growth of between 18,000 and 20,000 new student profiles a day.

The process described here is not hard, and it's not new—companies like Frog Design have been leveraging this approach for years, and I learned the fundamentals of empathetic design when I was an undergraduate at Carnegie Mellon. But for most companies, this process requires leaning on a different corporate ideology. It's a process informed by deep qualitative data rather than statistical market data. It celebrates people rather than technology. And it requires identifying and believing in behavioral insights, which are subjective and, in their ambiguity, full of risk.

JON KOLKO is the vice president of design at Blackboard, an education software company, the founder and director of Austin Center for Design, and the author of *Well-Designed: How to Use Empathy to Create Products People Love* (Harvard Business Review Press, 2014).

Note

1. R. Martin, *The Design of Business: Why Design Thinking Is the Next Competitive Advantage* (Boston: Harvard Business Review Press, 2009.)

Adapted from content posted on hbr.org
on April 23, 2015 (product #H0201E).

8

How Facebook Uses Empathy to Keep User Data Safe

By Melissa Luu-Van

Online security often focuses on technical details: software, hardware, vulnerabilities, and the like. But effective security is driven as much by people as it is by technology. After all, the point is to protect the consumers, employees, and partners who use our products.

The ways those people interact with technology and each other can completely change the effectiveness of your security strategy. So security products and tools must take into account the human context of the problems they're solving—and that requires empathy.

At Facebook, empathy helps us create solutions that work because they're designed around our users' experiences and well-being. Specifically, we see three ways to make security efforts more empathetic.

Consumer-driven goals that are actionable and specific. By researching the cultural and physical contexts in which people use the things you produce, you can define better, more precise goals for those products. Engaging with your users on a regular basis—through reporting tools built into your product, online surveys, or focus groups, for example—is a necessary step for understanding, rather than assuming you know, their challenges and needs.

For example, we recently asked several focus groups about their most important security concerns on Facebook. What are they worried about? What would help them feel safe? Overwhelmingly, people told us they wanted more control. Simply knowing that Facebook was working behind the scenes to protect their accounts wasn't enough. We learned that many Facebook users were unaware of all the security features we offer to add extra protection to their accounts. But once they learned about them, they were eager to use them. People also wanted to be able to control these features and to see how each tool protects their account. These findings told us two very important things about the security features. First, they needed to be easier to find. Second, they needed to be more visible and give people more control.

With that in mind, we created Security Checkup, a tool designed to make Facebook's security controls more visible and easier to use. During early testing and after our global launch, we asked people on Facebook about their experience using the new tool. They told us they found Security Checkup useful and helpful; the tool's completion rate quickly soared to over 90%. These results are validating—but not surprising, since we tailored Security Checkup to what we had learned about people's preferences and concerns.

Our primary goal has always been to protect the people who use Facebook, but through our research we've added the goal of helping people better protect themselves wherever they are on the web. The security lessons our users learn on Facebook could help them develop safer online habits—such as using unique passwords or checking app permissions—that can be used on other sites, too.

Collaborative, cross-functional teams. Security is often approached as an engineering-led effort in which cross-functional teams from research, design, or product are less important. However, we've found that disciplines besides engineering are just as critical to the thought process and product development, because diversity of thought is an important characteristic of empathy.

Cross-functional teams are particularly valuable for thinking through the various experiences people may have with a product. Car manufacturers have done this for years, adding seat belts and air bags to keep people safe even when a vehicle performs outside its intended purpose (that is, during a high-speed crash). The cars' designs were changed to make people's experiences safer by default. Similarly, Facebook's security tools are built with the belief that better product design leads to safer behavior. Many of our departments collaborate for this purpose, including research, security, user experience, marketing, product design, and communications.

Throughout various stages of the process, these teams convene to discuss potential engineering, design, or security challenges; identify solutions; and consider the impact any of these things might have on someone's overall experience using our products. We believe this collective expertise helps us avoid possible issues by addressing them early on in the development process. For example, during early iterations of Security Checkup we realized that simply drawing attention to our existing security features was interpreted by some people as a warning or alert that something was wrong. Because we had design and communication experts already working on the development team, we were able to create a security tool with a utilitarian tone to avoid making people feel unnecessarily concerned.

A focus on outcomes rather than inputs. Finally, and most important, empathy helps us keep people safe. If people don't have a safe experience, it doesn't matter how many security tools we make. That's why people's actual outcomes are always our highest priority. Empathy helps in a couple of ways.

First, having empathy for the people who use your products keeps you focused on helping them make small but useful tweaks (rather than major overhauls) to their online behavior. Because online security can be a daunting topic, many people shy away from being proactive about it. So encouraging people to start with small steps can go a long way. We've seen that even incremental progress helps people learn how to recognize risk and make safer choices. Simple behaviors like turning on extra security settings for online accounts can have a huge impact on someone's safety.

Second, using empathetic language in consumer communication makes security less intimidating and more accessible. This means using terms and concepts that are easily understood within local cultural and languages, even if they differ from the terms technical experts would use. Research shows that over time, fearful communications designed to scare people actually have a diminishing rate of return in helping consumers avoid online threats. On the other hand, building resiliency can help people better understand potential threats, recover from mistakes, and identify the most important preventative actions.

If you want to increase empathy on your team, one of the best ways to do it is to invite a diverse set of disciplines to be part of the product development process, both through hiring and through collaborating with other teams. Professionals with experience in psychology, behavioral sciences, or communications can bring invaluable perspectives for building an empathetic team. Then invest in research to understand the experience and security concerns of the people using your products; don't guess or assume you know what they are.

Empathy is not easy. It requires a commitment to deeply understanding the people you're protecting—but it also leads to significantly better security. And that's the whole point.

MELISSA LUU-VAN is a product manager at Facebook, where she leads a cross-functional team focused on helping people maintain access to their accounts and keep them secure.

Adapted from content posted on hbr.org
on April 28, 2016 (product #H02U0U).

9

The Limits
of Empathy

By Adam Waytz

A few years ago, Ford Motor Company started asking its (mostly male) engineers to wear the Empathy Belly, a simulator that allows them to experience symptoms of pregnancy first-hand—the back pain, the bladder pressure, the 30 or so pounds of extra weight. They can even feel "movements" that mimic fetal kicking. The idea is to get them to understand the ergonomic challenges that pregnant women face when driving, such as limited reach, shifts in posture and center of gravity, and general bodily awkwardness.

It's unclear whether this has improved Ford's cars or increased customer satisfaction, but the engineers claim benefits from the experience. They're still using the belly; they're also simulating the foggy vision and stiff joints of elderly drivers with an "age suit." If nothing more, these exercises are certainly an attempt to "get the other person's point of view," which Henry Ford once famously said was the key to success.

Empathy is all the rage pretty much everywhere—not just at Ford and not just on engineering and product development teams. It's at the heart of design thinking and innovation more broadly defined. It's also touted as a critical leadership skill—one that helps you influence others in your organization, anticipate stakeholders' concerns, respond to social media followers, and even run better meetings.

But recent research (by me and many others) suggests that all this heat and light may be a bit too intense. Though empathy is essential to leading and managing others—without it, you'll make disastrous decisions and forfeit the benefits just described—

failing to recognize its limits can impair individual and organizational performance.

Here are some of the biggest problems you can run into and recommendations for getting around them.

Problem #1: It's exhausting

Like heavy-duty cognitive tasks, such as keeping multiple pieces of information in mind at once or avoiding distractions in a busy environment, empathy depletes our mental resources. So jobs that require constant empathy can lead to "compassion fatigue," an acute inability to empathize that's driven by stress, and burnout, a more gradual and chronic version of this phenomenon.

Health and human services professionals (doctors, nurses, social workers, corrections officers) are especially at risk, because empathy is central to their day-to-day jobs. In a study of hospice nurses, for example, the key predictors for compassion fatigue were psychological: anxiety, feelings of trauma, life demands, and what the researchers call excessive empathy, meaning the tendency to sacrifice one's own needs for others' (rather than simply "feeling" for people).[1] Variables such as long hours and heavy caseloads also had an impact, but less than expected. And in a survey of Korean nurses, self-reported compassion fatigue strongly predicted their intentions to leave their jobs in the near future.[2] Other studies of nurses show additional consequences of compassion fatigue, such as absenteeism and increased errors in administering medication.

People who work for charities and other nonprofits (think animal shelters) are similarly at risk. Voluntary turnover is exceedingly high, in part because of the empathically demanding nature of the work; low pay exacerbates the element of self-sacrifice. What's more, society's strict views of how nonprofits should operate mean they face a backlash when they act like businesses (for instance, investing in "overhead" to keep the organization running smoothly). They're expected to thrive through selfless outpourings of compassion from workers.

The demand for empathy is relentless in other sectors as well. Day after day, managers must motivate knowledge workers by understanding their experiences and perspectives and helping them find personal meaning in their work. Customer service professionals must continually quell the concerns of distressed callers. Empathy is exhausting in any setting or role in which it's a primary aspect of the job.

Problem #2: It's zero-sum

Empathy doesn't just drain energy and cognitive resources—it also depletes itself. The more empathy I devote to my spouse, the less I have left for my mother; the more I give to my mother, the less I can give my son. Both our desire to be empathic and the effort it requires are in limited supply, whether we're dealing with family and friends or customers and colleagues.

Consider this study: Researchers examined the trade-offs associated with empathic behaviors at work and at home by surveying 844 workers from various sectors, including hairstylists, firefighters, and telecom professionals.[3] People who reported workplace behaviors such as taking "time to listen to coworkers' problems and worries" and helping "others who have heavy workloads" felt less capable of connecting with their families. They felt emotionally drained and burdened by work-related demands.

Sometimes the zero-sum problem leads to another type of trade-off: Empathy toward insiders—say, people on our teams or in our organizations—can limit our capacity to empathize with people outside our immediate circles. We naturally put more time and effort into understanding the needs of our close friends and colleagues. We simply find it easier to do, because we care more about them to begin with. This uneven investment creates a gap that's widened by our limited supply of empathy: As we use up most of what's available on insiders, our bonds with them get stronger, while our desire to connect with outsiders wanes.

Preferential empathy can antagonize those who see us as protecting our own (think about how people reacted when the Pope praised the Catholic Church's handling of sexual abuse). It can also, a bit more surprisingly, lead to insiders' aggression toward outsiders. For example, in a study I conducted with University of Chicago professor Nicholas Epley, we looked at how two sets of participants—those sitting with a friend (to prime empathic connection) and those sitting with a stranger—would treat a group of terrorists, an outgroup with particularly negative associations. After describing the terrorists, we asked how much participants endorsed statements portraying them as subhuman, how acceptable waterboarding them would be, and how much voltage of electric shock they would be willing to administer to them. Merely sitting in a room with a friend significantly increased people's willingness to torture and dehumanize.

Although this study represents an extreme case, the same principle holds for organizations. Compassion for one's own employees and colleagues sometimes produces aggressive responses toward others. More often, insiders are simply uninterested in empathizing with outsiders—but even that can cause people to neglect opportunities for constructive collaboration across functions or organizations.

Problem #3: It can erode ethics

Finally, empathy can cause lapses in ethical judgment. We saw some of that in the study about terrorists. In many cases, though, the problem stems not from aggression toward outsiders but, rather, from extreme loyalty toward insiders. In making a focused effort to see and feel things the way people who are close to us do, we may take on their interests as our own. This can make us more willing to overlook transgressions or even behave badly ourselves.

Multiple studies in behavioral science and decision making show that people are more inclined to cheat when it serves another person.[4] In various settings, with the benefits ranging from financial to reputational, people use this ostensible altruism to rationalize their dishonesty. It only gets worse when they empathize with another's plight or feel the pain of someone who is treated unfairly: In those cases, they're even more likely to lie, cheat, or steal to benefit that person.

In the workplace, empathy toward fellow employees can inhibit whistle-blowing—and when that happens, it seems scandals often follow. Just ask the police, the military, Penn State University, Citigroup, JPMorgan, and WorldCom. The kinds of problems that have plagued those organizations—brutality, sexual abuse, fraud—tend to be exposed by outsiders who don't identify closely with the perpetrators.

In my research with Liane Young and James Dungan of Boston College, we studied the effects of loyalty on people using Amazon's Mechanical Turk, an online marketplace where users earn money for completing tasks. At the beginning of the study, we asked some participants to write an essay about loyalty and others to write about fairness. Later in the study, they were each exposed to poor work by someone else. Those who had received the loyalty nudge were less willing to blow the whistle on a fellow user for inferior performance. This finding complements research showing that bribery is more common in countries that prize collectivism.[5] The sense of group belonging and interdependence among members often leads people to tolerate the offense. It makes them feel less accountable for it, diffusing responsibility to the collective whole instead of assigning it to the individual.

In short, empathy for those within one's immediate circle can conflict with justice for all.

How to rein in excessive empathy

These three problems may seem intractable, but as a manager you can do a number of things to mitigate them in your organization.

Split up the work

You might start by asking each employee to zero in on a certain set of stakeholders, rather than empathize with anyone and everyone. Some people can focus primarily on customers, for instance, and others on coworkers—think of it as creating task forces to meet different stakeholders' needs. This makes the work of developing relationships and gathering perspectives less consuming for individuals. You'll also accomplish more in the aggregate, by distributing "caring" responsibilities across your team or company. Although empathy is finite for any one person, it's less bounded when managed across employees.

Make it less of a sacrifice

Our mindsets can either intensify or lessen our susceptibility to empathy overload. For example, we exacerbate the zero-sum problem when we assume that our own interests and others' are fundamentally opposed. (This often happens in deal making, when parties with different positions on an issue get stuck because they're obsessed with the gap between them.) An adversarial mindset not only prevents us from understanding and responding to the other party but also makes us feel as though we've "lost" when we don't get our way. We can avoid burnout by seeking integrative solutions that serve both sides' interests.

Take this example: A salary negotiation between a hiring manager and a promising candidate will become a tug-of-war contest if they have different numbers in mind and fixate on the money alone. But let's suppose that the candidate actually cares more about job security, and the manager is keenly interested in avoiding turnover. Building security into the contract would be a win-win: an empathic act by the manager that wouldn't drain his empathy reserves the way making a concession on salary would, because keeping new hires around is in line with his own desires.

There's only so much empathy to go around, but it's possible to achieve economies of sorts. By asking questions instead of letting assumptions go unchecked, you can bring such solutions to the surface.

Give people breaks

As a management and organizations professor, I cringe when students refer to my department's coursework—on leadership, teams, and negotiation—as "soft skills." Understanding and responding to the needs, interests, and desires of other human beings involves some of the *hardest* work of all. Despite claims that empathy comes naturally, it takes arduous mental effort to get into another person's mind—and then to respond with compassion rather than indifference.

We all know that people need periodic relief from technical and analytical work and from rote jobs like data entry. The same is true of empathy. Look for ways to give employees breaks. It's not sufficient to encourage self-directed projects that also benefit the company (and often result in more work), as Google did with its 20% time policy. Encourage individuals to take time to focus on their interests alone. Recent research finds that people who take lots of self-focused breaks subsequently report feeling more empathy for others.[6] That might seem counterintuitive, but when people feel restored, they're better able to perform the demanding tasks of figuring out and responding to what others need.

How do you give people respite from thinking and caring about others? Some companies are purchasing isolation chambers like Orrb Technologies' wellness and learning pods so that people can literally put themselves in a bubble to relax, meditate, or do whatever else helps them recharge. McLaren, for example, uses the pods to train F1 supercar drivers to focus. Other companies, such as electrical parts distributor Van Meter, are relying on much simpler interventions like shutting off employee email accounts when workers go on vacation to allow them to concentrate on themselves without interruption.

Despite its limitations, empathy is essential at work. So managers should make sure employees are investing it wisely.

When trying to empathize, it's generally better to talk with people about their experiences than to imagine how they might be feeling, as Nicholas Epley suggests in his book *Mindwise*. A recent study bears this out.[7] Participants were asked how capable they thought blind people were of working and living independently. But before answering the question, some were asked to complete difficult physical tasks while wearing a blindfold. Those who had done the blindness simulation judged blind people to be much less capable. That's because the exercise led them to ask "What would it be like if *I* were blind?" (the answer: very difficult!) rather than "What is it like for *a blind person* to be blind?" This finding speaks to why Ford's use of the Empathy Belly, while well-intentioned, may be misguided: After wearing it, engineers may overestimate or misidentify the difficulties faced by drivers who actually are pregnant.

Talking to people—asking them how they feel, what they want, and what they think—may seem simplistic, but it's more accurate. It's also less taxing to employees and their organizations, because it involves collecting real information instead of endlessly speculating. It's a smarter way to empathize.

ADAM WAYTZ is an associate professor of management and organizations at Northwestern University's Kellogg School of Management.

Notes

1. M. Abendroth and J. Flannery, "Predicting the Risk of Compassion Fatigue: A Study of Hospice Nurses," *Journal of Hospice and Palliative Nursing* 8, no. 6 (November–December 2006): 346–356.

2. K. Sung et al., "Relationships Between Compassion Fatigue, Burnout, and Turnover Intention in Korean Hospital Nurses," *Journal of Korean Academy of Nursing* 42, no. 7 (December 2012): 1087–1094.

3. J. Halbesleben et al., "Too Engaged? A Conservation of Resources View of the Relationships Between Work Engagement and Work Interference with Family," *Journal of Applied Psychology* 94, no. 6 (November 2009): 1452–1465.

4. F. Gino et al., "Self-Serving Altruism? The Lure of Unethical Actions That Benefit Others," *Journal of Economic Behavior & Organization* 93 (September 2013); and F. Gino and L. Pierce, "Dishonesty in the Name of Equity," *Psychological Science* 20, no. 9 (December 2009): 1153–1160.

5. N. Mazar and P. Aggarwal, "Greasing the Palm: Can Collectivism Promote Bribery?" *Psychological Science* 22, no. 7 (June 2011): 843–848.

6. G. Boyraz and J. B. Waits, "Reciprocal Associations Among Self-Focused Attention, Self-Acceptance, and Empathy: A Two-Wave Panel Study," *Personality and Individual Differences* 74 (2015): 84–89.

7. A. M. Silverman et al., "Stumbling in Their Shoes: Disability Simulations Reduce Judge Capabilities of Disabled People," *Social Psychological & Personality Science* 6, no. 4 (May 2015): 464–471.

Reprinted from *Harvard Business Review*,
January–February 2016 (product #R1601D).

10

What the Dalai Lama Taught Daniel Goleman About Emotional Intelligence

An interview with Daniel Goleman by Andrea Ovans

Two decades before Daniel Goleman first wrote about emotional intelligence in the pages of HBR, he met the Dalai Lama at Amherst College. The Dalai Lama mentioned to the young science journalist for the *New York Times* that he was interested in meeting with scientists. Thus began a long, rich friendship as Goleman became involved over the years in arranging a series of what he calls "extended dialogues" between the Buddhist spiritual leader and researchers in fields ranging from ecology to neuroscience. Over the next 30 years, as Goleman has pursued his own work as a psychologist and business thinker, he has come to see the Dalai Lama as a highly uncommon leader. And so he was understandably delighted when, on the occasion of his friend's 80th birthday, he was asked to write a book describing the Dalai Lama's compassionate approach to addressing the world's most intractable problems. Published in June 2015, *Force for Good: The Dalai Lama's Vision for Our World*, which draws both on Goleman's background in cognitive science and his long relationship with the Dalai Lama, is both an exploration of the science and the power of compassion and a call to action. Curious about the book and about how the Dalai Lama's views on compassion informed Goleman's thinking on emotional intelligence, I caught up with Goleman over the phone. What follows are edited excerpts from our conversation.

HBR: *Let's start with some definitions here. What is compassion, as you are describing it? It sounds a lot like empathy, one of the major components of emotional intelligence. Is there a difference?*

Goleman: Yes, an important difference. As I've written about recently in HBR, three kinds of empathy are important to emotional intelligence: *cognitive empathy*—the ability to understand another person's point of view, *emotional empathy*—the ability to feel what someone else feels, and *empathic concern*—the ability to sense what another person needs from you [see chapter 1, "What Is Empathy?"]. Cultivating all three kinds of empathy, which originate in different parts of the brain, is important for building social relationships.

But compassion takes empathy a step further. When you feel compassion, you feel distress when you witness someone else in distress—and because of that you want to help that person.

Why draw this distinction?

Simply put, compassion makes the difference between understanding and caring. It's the kind of love that a parent has for a child. Cultivating it more broadly means extending that to the other people in our lives and to people we encounter. I think that in the workplace, that attitude has a hugely positive effect, whether it's in how we relate to our peers, how we are as a leader, or how we relate to clients and customers. A positive disposition toward another person creates the kind of resonance that builds trust and loyalty and makes interactions harmonious. And the opposite of that—when you do nothing to show that you care—creates distrust and disharmony and causes huge dysfunction at home and in business.

When you put it that way, it's hard to disagree that if you treat people well things would go better than if you don't or that if you cared about them they would care a lot more about you. So why do you think that doesn't just happen naturally? Is it a cultural thing? Or a misplaced confusion about when competition is appropriate?

I think too often there's a muddle in people's thinking that if I'm nice to another person or if I have their interests at heart it means that I don't have my own interests at heart. The pathology of that is, "Well, I'll just care about me and not the other person." And that, of course, is the kind of attitude that leads to lots of problems in the business realm and in the personal realm. But compassion also includes yourself. If we protect ourselves and make sure we're okay—and also make sure the other person is okay—that creates a different framework for working with and cooperating with other people.

Could you give me an example of how that might work in the business world?

There's research that was done on star salespeople and on client managers that found that the lowest level of performance was a kind of "I'm going to get the best deal I can now, and I don't care how this affects the other person" attitude, which

123

means that you might make the sale but that you lose the relationship. But at the top end, the stars were typified by the attitude, "I am working for the client as well as myself. I'm going to be completely straight with them, and I'm going to act as their advisor. If the deal I have is not the best deal they can get I'm going to let them know because that's going to strengthen the relationship, even though I might lose this specific sale." And I think that captures the difference between the "me first" and the "let's all do well" attitude that I'm getting at.

How would we cultivate compassion if we just weren't feeling it?

Neuroscientists have been studying compassion recently, and places like Stanford, Yale, UC Berkeley, and the University of Wisconsin, Madison, among others, have been testing methodologies for increasing compassion. Right now there's a kind of a trend toward incorporating mindfulness into the workplace, and it turns out there's data from the Max Planck Institute showing that enhancing mindfulness does have an effect in brain function but that the circuitry that's affected is not the circuitry for concern or compassion. In other words, there's no automatic boost in compassion from mindfulness alone.

Still, in the traditional methods of meditation that mindfulness in the workplace is based on, the two were always linked, so that you would practice mindfulness in a context in which you'd also cultivate compassion.

Stanford, for example, has developed a program that incorporates secularized versions of methods that have originally come from religious practices. It involves a meditation in which you cultivate an attitude of loving-kindness or of concern, or of compassion, toward people. First you do this for yourself, then for people you love, then for people you just know. And finally you do it for everyone. And this has the effect of priming the circuitry responsible for compassion within the brain so that you are more inclined to act that way when the opportunity arises.

You've remarked that the Dalai Lama is a very distinctive kind of leader. Is there something we could learn as leaders ourselves from his unique form of leadership?

Observing him over the years, and then doing this book for which I interviewed him extensively, and of course being immersed in leadership literature myself, three things struck me.

The first is that he's not beholden to any organization at all. He's not in any business. He's not a party leader. He's a citizen of the world at large. And this has freed him to tackle the largest problems we face. I think that to the extent that a leader is beholden to a particular organization or outcome, that creates a kind of myopia of what's possible and what matters. Focus narrows to the next quarter's results or the next election. He's way beyond that. He thinks in terms of generations and of what's best for humanity as a whole. Because his vision is so expansive, he can take on the largest challenges, rather than small, narrowly defined ones.

So I think there's a lesson here for all of us, which is to ask ourselves if there is something that limits our vision—that limits our capacity to care. And is there a way to enlarge it?

The second thing that struck me is that he gathers information from everywhere. He meets with heads of state, and he meets with beggars. He's getting information from people at every level of society worldwide. This casting a large net lets him understand situations in a very deep way, and he can analyze them in many different ways and come up with solutions that aren't confined by anyone. And I think that's another lesson everyday leaders can take from him.

The third thing would be the scope of his compassion, which I think is an ideal that we could strive for. It's pretty unlimited. He seems to care about everybody and the world at large.

You've said that the book is a call to action. What do you hope people will do after reading it?

The book is a call to action, but it is a very reasoned call to action. The Dalai Lama is a great believer in a deep analysis of problems and letting solutions come from that analysis. And then he is also passionate about people acting now. Not feeling passive, not feeling helpless, not feeling, "What's the point? I won't live to see the benefit," but rather having them start changes now even if the change won't come to fruition until future generations.

So my hope, and his, is to help people understand what they can do in the face of problems that are so vast: creating a more inclusive economy; making work meaningful; doing good and not just well; cleaning up injustice and unfairness, corruption and collusion in society, whether in business, politics, or religion; helping the environment heal; the hope that one day conflict will be settled by dialogue rather than war.

These are very big issues. But everyone can do something to move things in the right direction, even if it's just reaching across the divide and becoming friendly with someone who belongs to some other group. That actually has a very powerful end result: If you have two groups somewhere in the world that have deep enmity toward each other, and yet a few people in each group like each other because they've had personal contact—they have a friend in that other group. So something as simple as reaching out across a divide is actually a profound thing. In each of these areas, with whatever leverage we have, the point is to use it, not just to stand back.

DANIEL GOLEMAN is a codirector of the Consortium for Research on Emotional Intelligence in Organizations at Rutgers University, coauthor of *Primal Leadership: Leading with Emotional Intelligence* (Harvard Business Review Press, 2013), and author of *The Brain and Emotional Intelligence: New Insights* and *Leadership: Selected Writings* (More Than Sound, 2011). His latest book is *A Force For Good: The Dalai Lama's Vision for Our World* (Bantam, 2015). ANDREA OVANS is a former senior editor at *Harvard Business Review*.

Adapted from content published on hbr.org
on May 4, 2015 (product #H021KQ).

Index

Invaluable insights
always at your fingertips

With an All-Access subscription to
Harvard Business Review, you'll get
so much more than a magazine.

Exclusive online content and tools
you can put to use today

My Library, your personal workspace for sharing,
saving, and organizing HBR.org articles and tools

Unlimited access to more than 4,000 articles in the
Harvard Business Review archive

Subscribe today at hbr.org/subnow

The most important management ideas all in one place.

We hope you enjoyed this book from *Harvard Business Review*. For the best ideas HBR has to offer turn to HBR's 10 Must Reads Boxed Set. From books on leadership and strategy to managing yourself and others, this 6-book collection delivers articles on the most essential business topics to help you succeed.

HBR's 10 Must Reads Series

The definitive collection of ideas and best practices on our most sought-after topics from the best minds in business.

- Change Management
- Collaboration
- Communication
- Emotional Intelligence
- Innovation
- Leadership
- Making Smart Decisions

- Managing Across Cultures
- Managing People
- Managing Yourself
- Strategic Marketing
- Strategy
- Teams
- The Essentials

hbr.org/mustreads

Buy for your team, clients, or event.
Visit hbr.org/bulksales for quantity discount rates.

**Harvard
Business
Review**
Press